DESTINATION SPACE

A Visit to

MARS

David and Patricia Armentrout

A Crabtree Seedlings Book

CRABTREE
Publishing Company
www.crabtreebooks.com

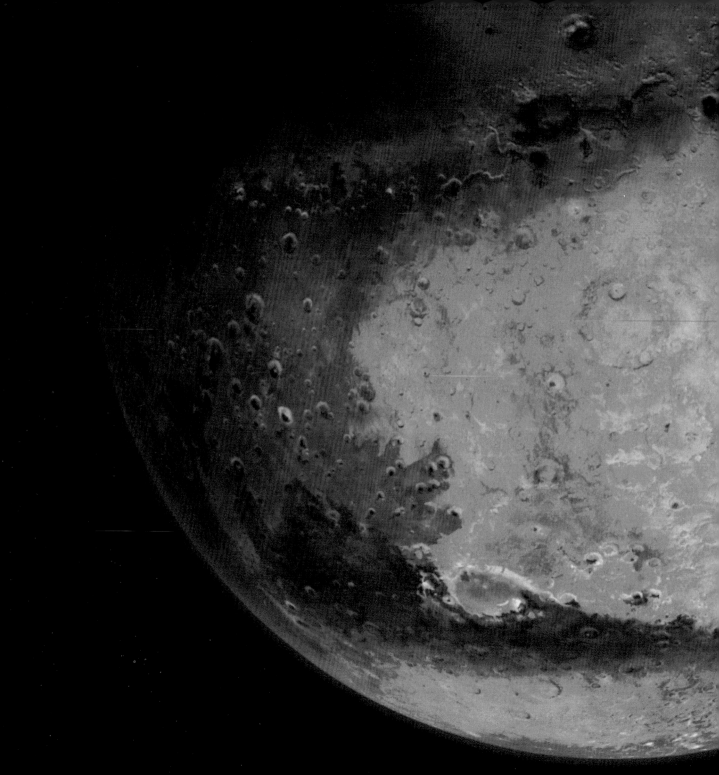

Table of Contents

Mars and our solar System

Our Sun is a medium-sized **star.**
It formed more than four billion years
ago. The Sun and all the objects that
orbit it make up our solar system.

Gravity is the force
that holds objects in
orbit around our Sun.

After the Sun, the eight largest objects in our solar system are **planets**. Mars is the fourth planet from the Sun.

Jupiter

Saturn

Uranus

Neptune

Comets, asteroids, and moons are also part of our solar system.

The first four planets from the Sun are rocky planets. Scientists call them terrestrial planets.

Mars is mostly rock and metals. Its surface is covered in a layer of iron oxide, or rust.

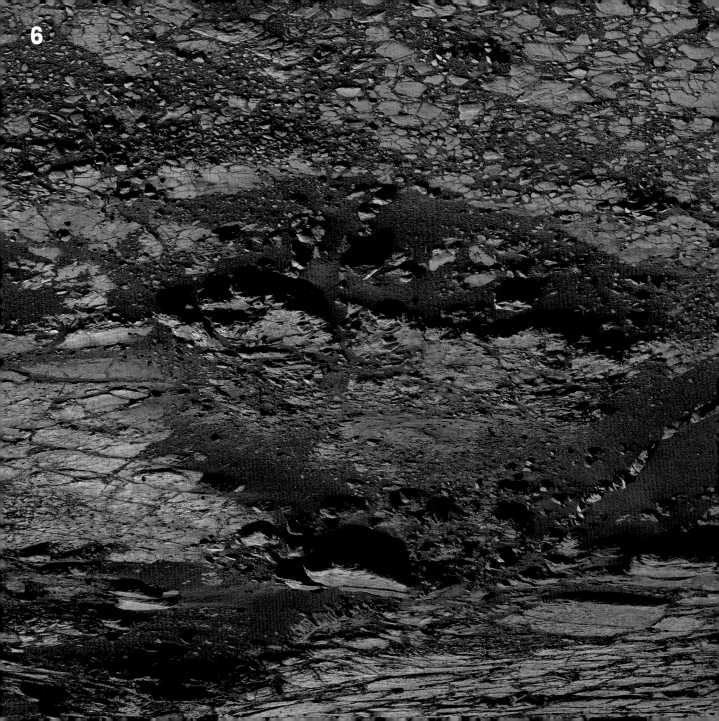

At night, Mars looks like a red star. From a distance, Mars appears red because rusty colored dust swirls around in its **atmosphere.** Up close, red-, brown-, tan-, and even green-colored soils are present.

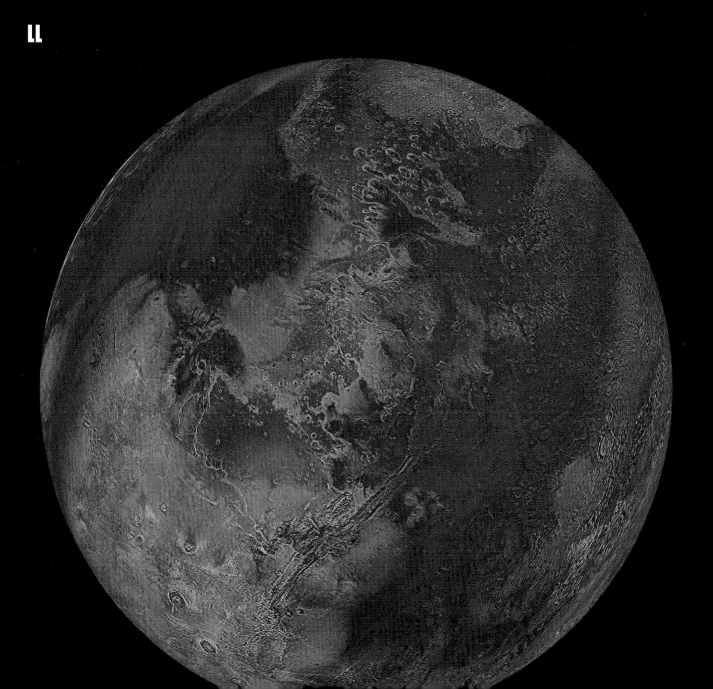

Mars and Earth— Neighbors in Space

The atmosphere of Mars is thinner than Earth's.

So, it is harder for Mars to hold onto the Sun's heat.

Mars, on average, is a colder planet than Earth.

Many objects in space have an atmosphere. Earth's atmosphere has the right combination of gases to support life.

Olympus Mons, a volcano on Mars, is the largest volcano in our solar system. At its base, *Olympus Mons* is about the size of Arizona!

Just like Earth, Mars has clouds, wind, and dust storms. Mars also has mountains and volcanoes. We know water does not flow on Mars today, but it does have icy polar caps like Earth.

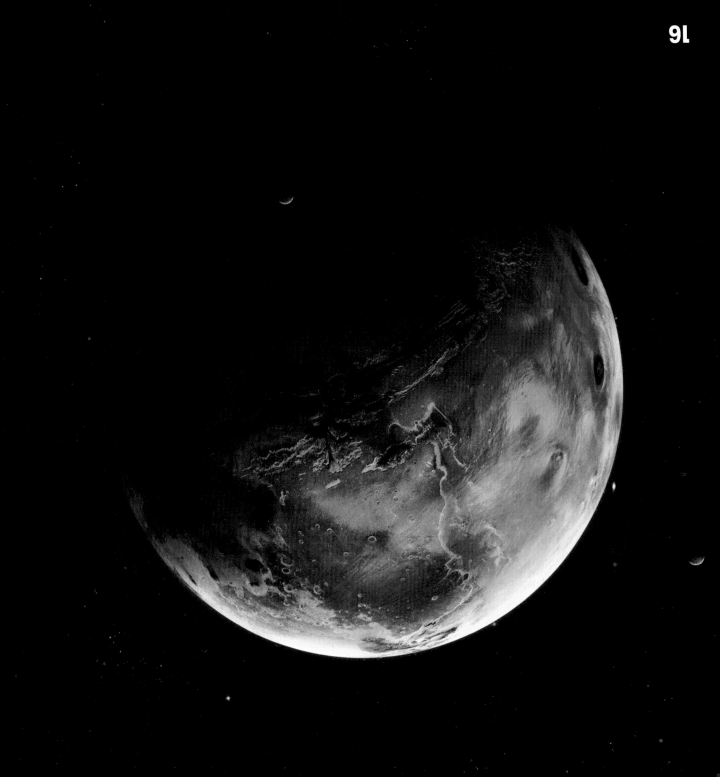

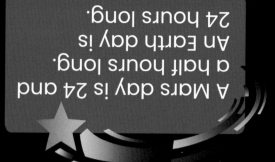

A Mars day is 24 and a half hours long. An Earth day is 24 hours long.

Mars, like Earth, spins on its **axis**. Because the two planets spin at about the same speed, their days are almost the same length. One complete turn, or spin, takes Mars 24 and a half hours.

Sun

Mercury

Venus

Earth

Mars is about 142 million miles
(228.5 million kilometers) from
the Sun. Earth is 93 million miles
(about 150 million kilometers)
from the Sun.

Mars and Earth have days that are similar, but their years are different. An Earth year is 365 days. This is how long Earth takes to orbit the Sun. It takes 687 Earth days for Mars to orbit the Sun.

Mars

Saturn

Neptune

Uranus

Jupiter

Curiosity rover

NASA's *Curiosity* rover has sent images to Earth from the surface of Mars.

Mission to Mars

Many spacecraft have visited Mars since the first mission was launched in the 1960s. Each time a spacecraft gets close, or lands, information about Mars is sent back to Earth.

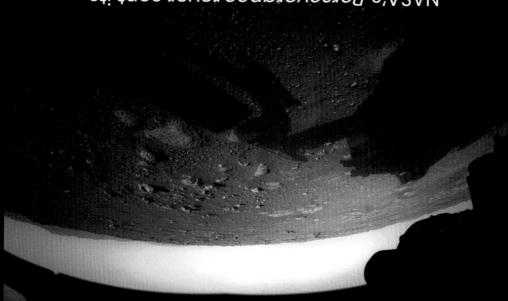

NASA's *Perseverance* rover sent its first color image from Mars in 2021.

Perseverance rover

In 2021, a new NASA rover, Perseverance, landed on Mars. Perseverance quickly began sending information to Earth. The information included images, video, and for the first time, sound.

Glossary

atmosphere (AT-muhss-fihr): A layer of gases around a planet.

axis (AKS-iss): An imaginary line about which a body, or planet, rotates.

NASA (NASA): Short for National Aeronautics and Space Administration. A branch of the government responsible for the research and exploration of space and space travel.

orbit (OR-bit): To travel in an invisible path around a larger object, such as a planet or star.

planets (Plan-its): Objects that travel around the Sun.

star (STAR): A ball of burning gases.

School-to-Home Support for Caregivers and Teachers

This book helps children grow by letting them practice reading. Here are a few guiding questions to help the reader build his or her comprehension skills. Possible answers appear here in red.

Before Reading
- **What do I think this book is about?** I think this book is about the planet Mars. I think this book is about being an astronaut and going to Mars.
- **What do I want to learn about this topic?** I want to learn about how Earth and Mars are the same and how they are different. I want to learn how long it takes for a rocket ship to get to Mars.

During Reading
- **I wonder why...** I wonder why Mars is known as the red planet. I wonder why no water flows on Mars.

- **What have I learned so far?** I have learned that the largest volcano in our solar system is on Mars. I have learned that a day on Mars is 24 and a half hours long.

After Reading
- **What details did I learn about this topic?** I have learned that it takes 687 Earth days for Mars to orbit the Sun. I have learned that in 2021 a new NASA rover, *Perseverance*, landed on Mars to send images, video, and sound back to Earth.
- **Read the book again and look for the glossary words.** I see the word *orbit* on page 4, and the word *atmosphere* on page 10. The other glossary words are found on page 23.

Library and Archives Canada Cataloguing in Publication

CIP available at Library and Archives Canada

Library of Congress Cataloging-in-Publication Data

CIP available at Library of Congress

Crabtree Publishing Company
www.crabtreebooks.com   1–800–387–7650

Written by: David and Patricia Armentrout
Production coordinator and Prepress technician: Tammy McGarr
Print coordinator: Katherine Berti

Printed in the U.S.A./CG20210915/012022

Print book version produced jointly with Blue Door Education in 2022

Content produced and published by Blue Door Education, Melbourne Beach FL USA. This title Copyright Blue Door Education. All rights reserved. No part of this book may be reproduced or utilized in any form or by any means, electronic or mechanical including photocopying, recording, or by any information storage and retrieval system without permission in writing from the publisher.

PHOTO CREDITS:
Cover © MarcelClemens ; star graphic on most pages © Gleb Guralnyk; pages 2-3 © ibreakstock, page 5 © Orla; page 6 © BlueRingMedia; page 8-9 © Bobboz; page 11, 14 and 15 © Ibooo7; page 13 © sebikus; page 16 and 19 © Webspark; page 17 © infografick; page 18 © beboy; page 21 © MarcelClemens; page 23 © Anton Balazh All images from Shutterstock.com

Published in the United States
Crabtree Publishing
347 Fifth Ave.
Suite 1402-145
New York, NY 10016

Published in Canada
Crabtree Publishing
616 Welland Ave.
St. Catharines, Ontario
L2M 5V6